CRACKPOT KINGS,

QUEENS

and other Daft Royals

Kay Barnham

WAYLAND

Published in paperback in 2016 by Wayland
Copyright © Hodder and Stoughton Limited 2016

Wayland is an imprint of Hachette Children's Group
Part of Hodder & Stoughton
Carmelite House
50 Victoria Embankment
London EC4Y 0DZ

Commissioned by: Debbie Foy
Design: Rocket Design (East Anglia) Ltd
Illustration: Alex Paterson
Proofreader/indexer: Susie Brooks

A catalogue for this title is available from
the British Library
352.2'3'0922

10 9 8 7 6 5 4 3 2 1

ISBN: 978 0 7502 8377 9

Printed in England

MIX
Paper from
responsible sources
FSC® C104740
www.fsc.org

An Hachette UK company
www.hachette.co.uk
www.hachettechildrens.co.uk

All illustrations by Shutterstock and Dover Publications, except:

11, 17, 27, 41, 46-7, 50-1, 62, 69, 89, 90

A GUIDE TO THE MODERN
BARMY-O-METER
(PATENT APPLIED FOR)

level 1: Mildly muddled

level 2: Slightly silly

level 3: Rather erratic

level 4: A bit bonkers

level 5: Completely ga-ga!

BARMY-O-METER

AS FEATURED IN THIS PUBLICATION!

How do our Kings, Queens and other Daft Royals rate on the Barmy-O-Meter?

Read on to find out!

ONCE UPON A ROYAL FAMILY

The crazy thing about kings, queens, princes, princesses, dukes, duchesses, archdukes, archduchesses, earls, countesses, barons and baronesses is that they don't apply for the job. There's no scary interview. They're born and – **BINGO** – they're royal.

Some people might marry into a royal family, of course, but in the past these were usually members of another royal family, which meant that they hadn't applied for that job either. Commoners – people without a noble rank or title – rarely turned into royals. It's all different now. **ANYONE** can marry a royal person. (As long as they like them, of course.)

Because they just inherited a title, this means that a lot of monarchs may not have been the right people for the job of being royal. Which is a shame, because there wasn't really any way of sacking them. (Unless they were Roman emperors, of course. Then they were just bumped off by whoever thought they deserved to be in power next.) And once they were king or queen or baroness or whatever, they were free to do pretty much what they liked.

4

Some royals chopped off people's heads. (That's you, Henry VIII.)

Some royals behaved in a really silly way. (Do you think 15,000 dresses might be a little excessive, Elizabeth of Russia ...?)

Some royals became so power-crazed that they thought they could do ANYTHING AT ALL and get away with it. (Just ask Ivan the Terrible.)

Sometimes, the history books make it sound as if a king or a prince or a duchess had totally lost the plot. But the crackpot things that the royals supposedly did might not have happened **EXACTLY** as people said. There might have been a little exaggeration here or a little storytelling there. Especially if the people who were reporting the stories wanted to find ways of making a monarch look silly so that they could overthrow them.

Crazy, huh?

The king who was just

Hello there, ladies!

Henry VIII of England (1491–1547)

The infamous Tudor king Henry VIII is famous for marrying not once, not twice, but a whopping SIX TIMES. And in Tudor times, this was pretty tricky, because divorce was illegal. So how did he do it…?

Henry VIII's first wife was Catherine of Aragon. She gave birth to a daughter, but that wasn't enough for Henry. He longed for a son and was fed up of waiting for one. So he asked the Roman Catholic Church if he could divorce her.

The Roman Catholic Church flatly refused.

MAD about MARRIAGE!

But did King Henry let that stop him? No. He simply got up one morning and started a new church called the Church of England. And because he was in charge of this church, he was able to do what he jolly well pleased. He divorced **Catherine of Aragon** and married **Anne Boleyn** instead.

BARMY RATING: 3 OUT OF 5

☞ Then Jane Seymour.

☞ Then Anne of Cleves.

☞ Then Catherine Howard.

☞ Then Catherine Parr.

And then he died, presumably from eating too much wedding cake.

✳ If you want to remember what happened to Henry VIII's wives, in the right order, just recite this handy rhyme:

Divorced, beheaded, died,
Divorced, beheaded, survived.

The lovestruck Tudors' club

WANTED:

SUITABLE WIFE FOR HENRY VIII

MUST LIKE...

Henry was a keen tennis player.

TENNIS

Oh, he could play the lute, too.

LUTE-PLAYING

Henry LOVED meat and dined on mutton, veal, venison, wild boar, peacock and swan.

MEAT

He was desperate for a son and heir.

GIVING BIRTH TO MALE HEIRS

TOILETS WITH LOADS OF SEATS

One of his toilets at Hampton Court Palace had 16 seats. But he had his own special plush loo, reserved for his royal bottom.

The small print

There is a very small chance that the king might get a little bit bored with you and want a royal divorce. But don't be upset if this happens because it's actually a good thing. The alternative is MUCH, MUCH worse. When Henry VIII gets REALLY fed up with a wife, he has a nasty habit of chopping her head off. Just ask Anne Boleyn or Catherine Howard.

8

CrackPot Quiz Question

Q. Did Henry VIII employ someone to ...?

a) wipe his nose;

b) wipe his chin after every meal;

c) wipe his bottom.

It's c), of course. Well, you wouldn't expect a king to wipe his own bottom, would you? It was a very important job, too. Not just anyone could be trusted to do it. Only the sons of noblemen need apply to be the 'groom of the stool'. Lucky them!

Emperor Qin Shi Huang of China (259 – 210BC)

This emperor feared death so much that he decided that an excellent way to avoid it would simply be to live for ever. (He survived three assassination attempts – so it's not surprising that he was worried about dying!) He spent his entire life searching for the key to immortality.

But that wasn't the only thing that scared the emperor. He also had a mortal fear of sea monsters. It's said that he caught pneumonia after hunting them. He didn't catch a sea monster, probably because they don't exist. And he didn't find a way of avoiding death either, because the pneumonia finished him off...

Or did it? There is another theory that Qin Shi Huang died after taking mercury pills prescribed by his doctors to make him 'immortal'. But as mercury is deadly poisonous, these would have killed him instead.

Either way, he died. BUT, as his tomb was guarded by the world-famous Terracotta Army – a collection of sculptures of warriors and horses that were supposed to protect him in his afterlife – he is definitely NOT forgotten.

BARMY RATING: 4 OUT OF 5

Hey, don't just ignore me!

Did They Really Do That?

Oh, I say! Excuse ME.

Roman emperor Elagabalus (203–222 AD) was a total minx at the dinner table. Instead of being regal and stately, he played tricks on his guests and was particularly fond of an early version of the whoopee cushion.

Parp!

The king who lost the plot... a lot

Charles IX of France (1550–1574)

Charles became king at just 10 years old, when his father Henry II died. It was a tricky time in France, when religious groups were warring, but Charles didn't have to worry about this, because even though he was the monarch, his mother was most definitely in charge. She was called Catherine de' Medici and she was very bossy. She told her son when to get up, when to eat, when to work, which political decisions to make, when go to church and probably when to blow his nose too. Charles was very obedient and did as he was told.

Did you leave the toilet seat up again, Charlie?

When he wasn't being bossed about, young Charles loved to go hunting – his mum went too, naturally – and he adored listening to and writing poetry. But what he hated more than anything else in the world was being told that he couldn't do something. If that happened, he lost his temper in a big way. In fact his tantrums were famous.

Sadly, the king died from tuberculosis when he was just 23. And when his brother Henry succeeded Charles to the throne, Catherine de' Medici simply told him what to do instead.

MAD ABOUT...
UNUSUAL PETS

Emperor Zhengde of China (1491–1521) built fabulous palaces – not for himself but for his pet tigers and leopards to live in!

The Russian tsar, Ivan the Terrible (1530–1584) was said to own two royal bears. But he didn't take them for walks, throw them sticks, let them sit on his lap or feed them treats. Oh no. He kept them locked up in a den in his castle and made sure that they were always hungry. That way, when he wanted to finish off a prisoner really quickly, he could throw him into the bears' den and be sure that the furry animals would gobble up the lot!

Emperor Nero (37–68 AD) owned a pet tiger called Phoebe and it's said that this was the only creature he ever loved. She lived in a golden cage, which was unlocked at mealtimes, so she could dine with the emperor.

Fig. 100: Camelus dromedarius

(It's a camel.)

Louis XIV of France (1638–1715) had two menageries, or private zoos. One was near his palace in Versailles where he kept hummingbirds, parrots, ostriches, a camel and an elephant. The king liked to invite artists and scientists to come and admire them. His other menagerie in Vincennes was a little different. This was where exotic animals such as tigers and elephants fought to their death for the amusement of his special guests. Luckily, this menagerie was closed in 1700 and the animals moved to Versailles.

Fig. 101: Ostrichius
(It's an ostrich.)

On his travels, Roman emperor Julius Caesar (100–44 BC) found a half-camel, half-leopard. (Or, as it is more usually known, a giraffe.) He took it back to Rome, where no one had ever seen such a creature. They had to be quick to catch a glimpse, though. Because Julius Caesar fed it to the lions in the Colosseum. Nice.

MAD, BAD
and truly sticky
ENDINGS

Fools!

Bum deal

Edmund II of England (989–1016), who fought a losing battle against the invading Danish king, Cnut the Great, was nicknamed Edmund Ironside because of his bravery on the battlefield. But Edmund didn't actually die on the battlefield. It was somewhere much less exciting. It's rumoured that poor old Edmund was stabbed up the bottom with a red-hot poker while he was sitting on the toilet.*

What a terrible way to go.

And now for toilet-related death number two. (Number two? **NUMBER TWO**? Geddit?! Oh, never mind.)

Spear of destiny

King Wenceslaus III of Bohemia (1289–1306) met a similar end to poor old Edmund II. When he was only 16, he was murdered with a spear while, again, sitting on the toilet!

It's a small wonder that any monarch dared to go to the loo in the Middle Ages ... Ouch!

Arghh!

BARMY-O-METER

BARMY RATING: 2 OUT OF 5

☞ * Others insist that he died of totally natural causes. But as he lived a whole millennium ago, official records are a little sketchy.

The TERRIBLY

Ivan IV Vasilyevich of Russia (1530 – 1584)

Ivan IV is better known as Ivan the Terrible* because he inspired terror wherever he went. But what did the Russian tsar actually **DO** to get this reputation…?

➤ After his favourite architects, Postnik and Barma, designed St Basil's Cathedral in Moscow, it is rumoured that Ivan had them blinded. He never wanted the men to design anything so wonderful ever again.

➤ He had an awful temper. Once, he got so mad he killed his own son.

➤ Suspecting that Russian nobles had poisoned his wife Anastasia, Ivan punished them. A lot.

➤ He told everyone that he no longer wanted to be king and then, when the Russians begged him to rethink, he agreed, but only on the condition that he had even more power than ever before.

➤ He created an elite – and very, very scary – police force. They wore black, rode black horses and specialised in torture and execution.

➤ When he got fed up with a wife, he just sent her to a convent and married a new one.

SCARY monarch

➤ He personally supervised a massacre in Novgorod, where he suspected the citizens of treason.

But Ivan the Terrible loved reading ... so he can't have been **ALL** bad.

> Oh yeah? You should see some of his books - 'How to blind an architect' - NOT nice!

☞ *In Russian, Ivan IV is known as Ivan Grozny (Ива́н Гро́зный), but although 'grozny' is often translated as 'terrible', it doesn't mean that Ivan was terrible at what he did. He was actually very, very good at being a powerful tsar. In fact, 'terrible' sometimes means 'causing terror'. So, Ivan the Terrible really means that he scared the pants off everyone. Either way, it was probably not a good idea to upset him.

Did They Really Do That?

'It is legal because I wish it.'

Look at my lovely hair.

Big head!

Louis XIV of France (1638–1715)

Wow. How big-headed. No monarch would be daft enough to say something like that today. And besides, it's usually governments and not kings or queens that make the laws nowadays. So it just wouldn't be legal!

Louis XIV

The glass king

Charles VI of France (1368–1422)

Poor Charles VI of France thought he was made of glass and was so worried that he would smash into pieces that he never did anything remotely dangerous. The king had iron rods sewn into his clothes so that if he fell over, he would not break. He even refused to travel by coach in case the bumpy roads made him shatter.

BARMY RATING: 4.5 OUT OF 5

Bonkers!

The poet-king of Seville

King Muhammad Ibn Abbad Al Mu'tamid of Seville (1040–1095)

King Mu'tamid wasn't just the monarch who ruled Seville, in Spain, and fought over nearby Cordoba a few times. He was a top poet too (actually, one of the best Andalusian poets ever). But there was yet another side to him – he was also a total, slushy, gooey, softy romantic. When he discovered that his wife had never seen snow, he had a whole hillside planted with almond trees. Confused? Aha. The reason he did this was that in springtime he knew that the trees would blossom and that the tumbling petals would look like snowflakes as they fell.

Awwww...

If you want to impress the one you love next Valentine's Day, why not try this yourself? All you need is your own hill and a forest of almond trees and enough money to pay for them. On second thoughts, why not just send a card.

BARMY RATING: 1 OUT OF 5

MAD ABOUT...
☞ THE EMPEROR OF CHINA

Elizabeth Monck, The Duchess of Albemarle (1654–1734)

After the Duke of Albemarle died, the Duchess of Albemarle decided that her next marriage would be into a VERY royal family. She soon became utterly convinced that the Kangxi Emperor of the Qing Dynasty in China wanted to marry her. The problem was that she'd never met him. And he lived over 8,000 kilometres away in China. He probably didn't know she even existed.

However, the First Duke of Montagu had met the duchess, because he was her sister-in-law's stepfather. And he lived in England, like her. So, the Duke of Montagu did a bad and utterly bonkers thing. He dressed up as the Kangxi Emperor of China and proposed to the Duchess of Albemarle. She fell head over heels in love with him, accepted the proposal and they were married in 1692.

The emperor who wasn't

Emperor Norton I of the USA (1819–1880)

Joshua Abraham Norton was a British man who declared himself emperor of the USA (and protector of Mexico) in 1859. He announced that the US Congress was to be abolished. The US Congress ignored him. He announced that the Democratic and Republican parties were to be abolished. They ignored him too. And then he announced the formation of a League of Nations, which actually happened, but not until 1919, which was 39 years after his death. He also demanded that there should be a bridge linking San Francisco to Oakland ... and this was actually built in the 1930s!

But whether he was emperor or not, the people of San Francisco loved him. Even though Norton was very broke, he ate at all of the best restaurants, for free. And when he died, it's reported that 30,000 people went to his funeral to pay their respects.

Sorry Sir, it's tickets only for the funeral.

Kublai Khan, Emperor of Mongolia (1215–1294)

Kublai Khan might have been the grandson of Genghis Khan – the fierce warrior leader who founded and ruled the Mongol Empire – but he was famous in his own right, too. He invaded China and started the Yuan Dynasty, which ruled both Mongolia and China for nearly a century.

Meanwhile, when Kublai Khan wasn't busy invading China, he liked to relax by doing something altogether less violent ... stargazing. But as he was a very powerful emperor, he didn't make do with looking at the night sky like a normal person.

He built actual star-gazing observatories. A whopping 27 of them, to be precise.

Army of GIANTS

Frederick William I of Prussia (1688 – 1740)

The King of Prussia* **LOVED** a good military display – the bigger the better. And he liked his soldiers to be big, too. Really big. In fact, he formed his own special giant regiment called the Potsdam Grenadiers.

YOUR COUNTRY NEEDS YOU

(But only if you're over 1.88 metres – 6 feet 2 inches – tall and don't mind wearing a uniform with a silly red hat, scarlet breeches, a Prussian blue jacket with gold lining and, um, white tights.)

Soon, the regiment became known as the Potsdam Giants, because they really were very big indeed, some as tall as 2.17 metres (7 feet). Frederick hired soldiers from all over Europe, by fair means and foul. No one was safe, not even priests. If a man didn't want to join Frederick's regiment, he simply had them kidnapped. By the time he died, there were 3,200 Potsdam Giants.

The bizarre thing was that poor Frederick was terribly short. At just 1.6 metres (5 feet 3 inches), he'd never have been able to join his own regiment.

* This is NOT a dodgy spelling of Russia, but an actual German kingdom that existed from 1525 to 1947. Prussia sprawled across a lot of Europe and included parts of modern Germany, Poland, Lithuania, Denmark, Belgium, the Czech Republic, Switzerland and, yes, OK ... parts of Russia too. But it wasn't Russia, all right?

The royal shocker

IT'S A RIGHT ROYAL READ!

ÆTHELRED THE UNREADY WAS READY

It's been revealed that King Æthelred (968–1016), who ruled over Saxon England, and who has long been criticised for being 'unready' actually wasn't unready, at all. It's just that his name was translated wrongly from Old English. Unfortunately for him, the name stuck.

It turns out that Æthelred, whose name means 'good counsel', was nicknamed Unræd because it means 'without counsel'. This is because he was given a lot of VERY SILLY advice, particularly on how he should run the country.

But he can't really be blamed for following the advice he was given. The poor lad was only 10 years old when he first came to the throne. And he can't actually have been that unready either, because he did manage to repel Vikings for most of his reign. And they were notoriously tricky to deal with.

A Viking – very similar to those repelled by Æthelred.

READ ON!

Was Richard III really an evil megalomaniac or was he just misunderstood? Turn to page 38 to find out!

Did They Really Do That?

> 'I am the emperor and I want dumplings!'

Emperor Ferdinand I of Austria
(1793–1875)

And it wasn't just any old dumplings that Ferdinand wanted. It was apricot dumplings. He loved them. And when his cook told him that he couldn't have his usual dumplings this week because apricots were out of season, he went totally beserk!

It's just not fair!

(He didn't get them, obviously. Not even emperors are powerful enough to make apricots grow on trees in the middle of winter.)

CrackPot
Quiz Question

Q. What did Princess Charlotte of Belgium and Empress Carlota of Mexico have in common ...?

a) They both had an unhealthy obsession with cheese;

b) They were the same person;

c) They were both great-grand-daughters of Catherine the Great.

It's b). And actually, she was briefly Archduchess Charlotte of Austria too. So how did she get to be two different people ...?

Princess Charlotte of Belgium married Archduke Maximilian of Austria in 1857. And when Napoleon III wanted to turn Mexico into a satellite state, he needed a figurehead for the country, so he asked Charlotte's husband to take on the role. Charlotte went too, and even changed her name to Carlota, which is Spanish for Charlotte. They were crowned Emperor and Empress Consort of Mexico in 1864. But the Mexican monarchy was doomed when Napoleon withdrew his troops. Carlota returned to Europe to gather support for her husband, but he was killed by his opponents in Mexico. She never got over it and she never went back.

MAD, BAD
and truly sticky
ENDINGS

Fools!

Béla I of Hungary (1016 – 1063)

Throne of doom

Béla I had a **VERY TALL, VERY WOODEN** and **VERY HEAVY** throne. Unfortunately, after it was cunningly sabotaged by enemies who wanted to get rid of him and rule Hungary instead, the throne collapsed when the king sat on it and Béla I was **VERY DEAD.**

The bell ringer

Fyodor I Ivanovich of Russia (1557–1598)

Fyodor never expected to be a Russian tsar. That should have been his elder brother Ivan. But when his father, Ivan the Terrible, argued with his son and heir, then killed him in a fit of temper, it meant that Fyodor was now next in line for the throne.

Poor old Fyodor was a gentle soul, who had no interest at all in being a tsar. Given the choice between ruling Russia and enjoying his all-time favourite hobby of bell ringing, the church bells won every time.

I'd rather be a campanologist, thanks!

BARMY-O-METER

BARMY RATING: 1 OUT OF 5

32

MAD ABOUT...
☞ BOILED EGGS ☞

King Louis XV of France
(1710 – 1774)

King Louis XV was a big fan of boiled eggs. He ate them A LOT, and because he ate so many, he developed a love of eggcups, too. He asked his court jewellers to make really lavish eggcups – which presumably made a change from making boring old diamond necklaces – and used these during breakfast and brunch meetings, where he often made his most important royal decisions.

Louis XV's party piece was beheading* a boiled egg with one swipe.

Fig. 99: Boildus Eggus

* Unfortunately, that's exactly what happened to his grandson Louis XVI in 1793, when he became the only French king ever to be sent to the dreaded guillotine!

A right royal fashionista

Elizabeth of Russia (1709 – 1762)

Elizabeth of Russia, a popular empress, had a passion for fashion. This is how much Elizabeth loved dressing up.

- She owned 15,000 dresses.

- She owned nearly as many pairs of shoes.

- She owned so many pairs of stockings that no one ever had time to count them.

- She never wore the same dress twice.

- She changed her outfit up to **SIX TIMES A DAY**.

- (So did her courtiers!)

- To make sure that no one wore the same dress more than once, at each ball, every gown was stamped with Elizabeth's special royal ink.

- She was determined to be so totally, utterly, perfectly unique that she introduced a law banning anyone else from wearing the same dress, the same hairdo or even the same accessory as her.

She also made it law that French designers had to offer her their newest fabrics before anyone else. Or else ...

Any woman who dared to be more beautiful than Elizabeth of Russia sent her **TOTALLY** crazy with jealousy.

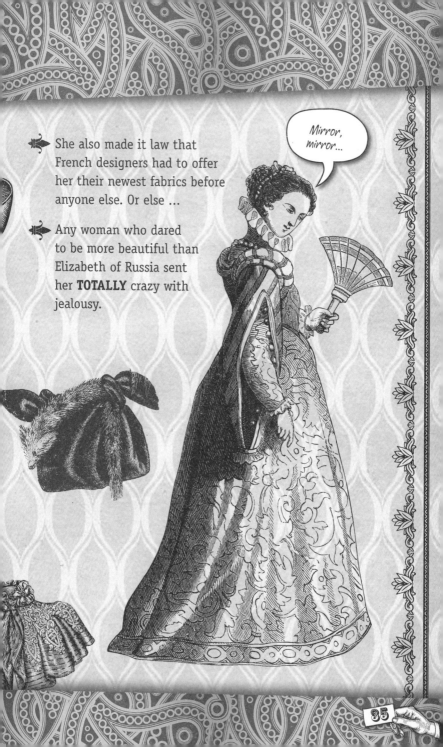

Mirror, mirror...

MADE-UP MONARCHS

The Queen of Hearts

She's not a proper queen, of course. The Queen of Hearts is one of the best-known characters from Lewis Carroll's *Alice's Adventures in Wonderland*. Despite her wonderfully charming name, she's fabulously angry. The Queen of Hearts doesn't just get mad, she gets REALLY, REALLY MAD, at anything and everything. A lot. And whenever someone makes her cross, the Queen of Hearts shouts, 'OFF WITH THEIR HEADS!'* She also enjoys playing croquet with a flamingo instead of a mallet and a hedgehog instead of a ball. As you do.

The Queen of Hearts is based on a real playing card. But in the book's illustrations, she's a proper 3D queen. It's been suggested that her character was inspired by the real-life Queen Victoria, but there is no evidence at all that

Queen Victoria ever commanded a beheading. So maybe this is not true.

Alice's Adventures in Wonderland is the tale of a girl who falls down a rabbit hole into a whole other world. She meets talking animals like the White Rabbit and the Cheshire Cat, finds a drink that makes her shrink and a cake that makes her — well, that would be telling. Read it yourself and find out. It's wonderfully bonkers.

☜ * Don't worry. No one actually loses their head in *Alice's Adventures in Wonderland*. As soon as the Queen of Hearts looks the other way, the King of Hearts – her much nicer husband – pardons them.

The royal shocker

Richard III REVEALED

In shocking new developments, it's been revealed that Richard III (1452–1485) may not have been as despicable as historians thought. King of England for just two paltry years, he's long been regarded as an evil, hunchback murderer, but it turns out that he may actually have been an OK sort of chap.

Was he a hunchback? NO

Experts suspect that he suffered from scoliosis. Sufferers have a curved spine and in Richard III's case this would have made one shoulder look as if it were higher than the other. He wasn't a hunchback.

How about the two princes in the Tower? NEVER PROVEN

It's long been suspected that Richard III murdered his own nephews – Prince Edward and Prince Richard – because they were next in line to the throne and he wanted to be king instead. But there's no proof.

So why did he have such a bad press? FRAMED

Richard III's bad press didn't really start until AFTER he died at the Battle of Bosworth in 1485. Tudor king Henry VII wanted to look good, so they made sure that the old king looked EXTREMELY bad, depicting him as a power-mad tyrant.

IT'S A RIGHT ROYAL READ!

And Shakespeare?

HE JUST WANTED TO TELL A GOOD STORY

He just joined in. *Richard III*, the play, was written in 1591, more than a century after the king's death. Shakespeare was hardly an eyewitness. So maybe Richard III didn't say:

And thus I clothe my naked villany
With old odd ends stolen out of holy writ;
And seem a saint, when most I play the devil.

Richard III, relaxing at home.

Right Royal Weather Report

TODAY'S WEATHER WILL BE CLOUDY WITH A CHANCE OF REIGN!

— STOP PRESS! —

A skeleton suspected to be that of Richard III was discovered **UNDER A CAR PARK** in Leicester in 2012. DNA tests revealed that it was the king and seeing as a car park – although it was a very nice car park – wasn't the most regal place to bury a king, it was decided to bury him in a cathedral and give him a proper royal send-off instead.

The fairytale king...

Ludwig II of Bavaria (1845–1886)

Once upon a time there was a king called Ludwig. Handsome, stylish and shy, Ludwig II of Bavaria spent so much time carrying out dull kingly duties that he yearned to feel like a real royal in a real fairytale castle. So he built one. Then another. And then a third. The problem was, keeping up this kind of royal lifestyle was very expensive. And when the banks stopped lending him money, the party was over.

Ludwig's fairytale castles:

Neuschwanstein*

Schloß (the German word for 'castle') Neuschwanstein is perched on top of a pointy hill in Bavaria, Germany. It is beautiful both inside and out, with turrets and towers on top and a theatre for guests inside. You can check it out in the film version of *Chitty Chitty Bang Bang* (1968). Or see the fabulous illustration of it opposite!

Herrenchiemsee

Ludwig wanted to build his very own version of the Palace of Versailles, near Paris, France. Herrenchiemsee has a hall of mirrors and formal gardens, like Versailles. But unlike Versailles, when it was first built, Herrenchiemsee had central heating AND toilets.

Linderhof

This is the smallest of Ludwig's palaces and the only one to be completed before he died, but it is still magnificent. Inside Linderhof, there are jewel-encrusted mantelpieces, an ivory candelabra, another hall of mirrors and an ostrich-plume carpet.

Ludwig II planned more fabulous castles, but they were never built. Ooh. How posh!

* The author, who has admired this very castle from the foot of the hill in real life, can confirm that it is indeed 'very pretty' and 'probably the most famous fairytale castle in the world'. But she didn't go on the tour because that was 'very expensive'. Much like Ludwig II's tastes.

CrackPot
Quiz Question

Q. After a trip to Europe, what did Peter the Great of Russia (1672–1725) insist that his courtiers remove …?

a) Their coats when they went into a warm room, so they would be sure to 'feel the benefit' when they went outside;

b) Their beards, because he'd suddenly decided that facial hair looked rubbish;

c) Their left eyebrow before they went into battle, for luck.

It was b). All the European men that Peter the Great met were clean-shaven and he decided that if the Russians wanted to look as cool as the Europeans, they should remove their long beards. He even made it law and beards were officially banned. But he wasn't a total meanie. Any man who really wanted to keep his beard could … if he paid an annual beard tax of 100 roubles.

An ELECTRIFYINGLY silly idea

Tsar Nicholas II of Russia (1868 – 1918)

It's rumoured that Nicholas II once decided it would be a wonderful idea to build an electric fence around his country. Whether this was to stop his fellow Russians from getting out or to stop people from other countries from getting in, or if he was thinking of investing in an **ENORMOUS** flock of sheep is unclear. But whatever the reason, it was never done.

Nicholas II also had the totally mad idea of building a bridge across the Bering Strait, which is the 85-kilometre-wide stretch of very icy water between Russia and the USA. That never happened either.

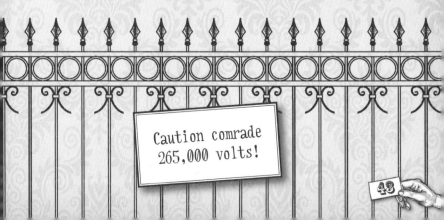

Caution comrade
265,000 volts!

43

Was he mad? Was he bad? Or was he just plain useless ...?

Henry VI of England (1421 – 1471)

When Henry V died, his son was just nine months old and FAR too young to be king of England. So Henry VI wasn't crowned until he reached the age of eight. Luckily, those in charge realised that this was still a bit young to be ruling an entire country, so they looked after England until Henry turned 16.

But even at 16, Henry VI still wasn't up to the challenge. He wasn't that interested in ruling and he wasn't any good at it, either. Plus, he chose the wrong advisors. When Henry married the French Margaret of Anjou, she started to boss him around too and things got even more complicated for him.

Henry VI is often blamed for the Wars of the Roses. This was a series of wars between the royal houses of Lancaster (symbolised by a red rose) and York (the white rose), who both thought they should be in charge of England. But although he might have been totally useless at ruling, several of his clever advisers didn't help matters. Besides, the problems that led to the civil war happened before he was even born, so it can't have been all his fault.

Henry VI was imprisoned in the Tower of London and died there in 1471, presumed murdered. Whatever mistakes he did make, he certainly didn't deserve that!

I'm really not sure that I'm cut out to be king, you know.

A right royal

Edward de Vere, 17th Earl of Oxford (1550 – 1604)

The Earl of Oxford became famous as the person who bowed and accidentally trouser-trumpeted in front of a queen. But that didn't make him a daft royal. That was the fact that, overcome by shame, he left the court AND the country and spent seven years travelling. Seven years! He hoped that was long enough for Queen Elizabeth I to forget the embarrassing episode. But no...

According to John Aubrey, who was a 17th-century biographer, the clever queen recognised the earl at once. 'My Lord,' she said. 'I had forgott* the Fart.'

Oh no, not now!

Take cover!

raspberry

Did They Really Do That?

How tall? How rude!

It's said that Edward VII of the United Kingdom (1841-1910) insisted on measuring how tall every one of his visitors was. Though, seeing as he was the monarch, he was far too important for such shenanigans and probably got someone else to do it. The measurement was then recorded.

He might have been king, but it was the height of bad manners!

Fools!

MAD, BAD
and truly sticky
ENDINGS

Charles II of Navarre (1349 – 1387)

Think yourself lucky that you never visited Charles II of
Navarre's doctor in 1387. When the 52-year-old king (who
ruled the tiny kingdom of Navarre in the Pyrenees, France)
was suffering from a mystery illness, his trusty medic didn't
prescribe medicine. Oh no. Presumably, that would have been
too obvious. Instead, he told a nurse to wrap poorly Charles in
linen cloth that had been SOAKED IN BRANDY.

The medicinal benefits of this bizarre treatment are uncertain.
Perhaps the linen and the brandy would have done the trick
and Charles would have had a miraculous recovery and gone on
to rule for another 52 years. Perhaps not. The fact is, the linen
and the brandy didn't get a chance to work because the nurse
who was wrapping the patient in bandages accidentally set light
to the (highly inflammable) cloth with a candle and the king
went up in flames.

The Grand Vizier of Persia (10th century)

Maybe there's a book you're reading that is so utterly brilliant that you like to carry it around with you, just in case you get a spare moment to read? Great. That's what the Grand Vizier of Persia did, too. Except, he didn't have just one favourite book. He had 117,000 of them. And because he couldn't bear to be parted with any of them, wherever he went, he insisted that his books went too. He needed to find a way of transporting his beloved library.

So it was loaded onto ... 400 CAMELS!

What's more, so that the bookaholic Vizier could find any book he wanted at any time, some camels carried the As, some the Bs and so on. And the clever camels were trained to walk in alphabetical order.

Thank goodness they didn't get the hump.

What have I told you about trying to overtake? Honestly, we're meant to be in alphabetical order!

Coming through, slowcoach!

The two-faced emperor

Caligula (12AD – 41AD)

Caligula became Roman emperor in 37AD, when he was 25. Thousands of animals were sacrificed in the three-month party that kick-started his reign, which showed that his citizens must have liked him. He was said to be a noble ruler, who hosted splendid games for his fellow Romans to enjoy. He brought back proper elections and he got rid of the sales tax. Everything was going well. But after an illness, Caligula changed totally.

The all-new Caligula now insisted that he was treated as a god. He became cruel and extravagant. He spent HUGE amounts of money on fancy construction projects. And he had a lot of very important people executed.

Caligula was stabbed to death by his own bodyguards when he was just 29. The Roman people were sad because he'd treated them well. Those in charge, not so much...

This is my cruel face. Do you want to see my cheeky face?

GALIGVLA · CÆS · AVG · IIII · RO · IM

MAD ABOUT...
BLING

The Prince Regent (1762–1830)

The Prince Regent* was larger than life. He dressed flamboyantly. He partied wildly. And he just loved extravagance, whether he was wearing it or hanging it on the walls of his glorious Royal Pavilion in Brighton. This was the Prince Regent's holiday home. And it was AMAZING. The onion-shaped domes, finials (pointy bits on top of the domes), arches and decorations are typical of the Indo-Saracenic style of architecture, which was very popular in late-19th-century British India. Although many of the original fixtures and fittings were removed and sent to other royal palaces after Prince Regent's death, it has been restored. And it's very lavish and totally magnificent.

* The Prince Regent was George III's son. When the king's odd behaviour meant that he could no longer rule, his son became a sort of caretaker king. But because he wasn't the actual king, he was called the Prince Regent. When George III (page 56) died, the Prince Regent became king at last and was then known as George IV.

Turn over for more bling

MAD ABOUT...
MORE BLING!

Peek inside some of the rooms of the Royal Pavilion...

The Music Room is where the Prince Regent's own band entertained guests. It has sumptuous red and gold canvasses hanging on the walls and the stunning domed ceiling is covered with hundreds of plaster cockleshells. Oh, and it's painted gold, of course. The Prince Regent was far too grand for plain old beige.

The Banqueting Room is probably the most lavish dining room in the world. The centrepiece is a glittering 9-metre-tall chandelier that hangs from the claws of a silvered dragon. It's not the sort of thing you'd usually find in your average DIY store.

The Great Kitchen is bigger than most houses. It had the very latest steam-heating technology and a fresh water supply. (But not a microwave.) Cast-iron columns decorated with copper palm leaves support the ceiling.

The Long Gallery is SO much posher than the average hall. The walls are painted with a leafy outdoor scene against a pink background. The ceiling is made of glass. Perhaps the Prince Regent got bored of gold.

The cost of being fabulous

All of this sumptuousness and splendour cost money, of course. Public money. And even though Parliament increased the Prince Regent's allowance in the 1780s, by 1795 he owed almost £50,000,000 in today's money. Reluctantly, Parliament agreed to bail him out IF he married Princess Caroline of Brunswick. So he did. (They didn't get on.) And then he carried on spending.

The Prince Regent's coronation at Westminster Abbey in 1821 was a fabulously magnificent event with a price tag to match. It cost a staggering £19,000,000 in today's money.

But his extravagant lifestyle didn't just cost money. It cost the Prince Regent his health, too. By 1824, his waist measured a button-popping 130 centimetres.

He died aged 57, a mere 10 years after ascending the throne.

The madness of King

George III of Great Britain and Ireland (1738–1820)

George III was supposedly the most crackpot king ever. He is famous for being on the throne while the American War of Independence and the Napoleonic Wars took place, but he is perhaps even more famous for his odd behaviour and his wild outbursts. Many declared him mad and for the last 10 years of George's life, his son the Prince Regent was put in charge in his place. Except, George III wasn't mad at all … in fact, he was **POISONED**.

It wasn't until this century that medical experts worked it out. First, they realised that the king's dark-red urine meant that he probably suffered from a rare disease called porphyria. This explained his strange behaviour. But then they wondered why his symptoms had got a lot worse as he grew older. And because they couldn't dig up the king to find out more, they tested strands of George's actual hair instead. (Handily, these had been kept safe in the vaults of a London museum.)

What the experts found was that the king's hair was filled with poisonous arsenic, which meant that the rest of his body must have been filled with arsenic, too. And as arsenic is known to bring on attacks of porphyria, the mystery of George III's madness was solved. Hurray!

George III's medicine

But just one question remained: **WHY** did George III happen to be filled with poison?

He was known to be a healthy eater, who took plenty of exercise. He went to bed early. He didn't throw wild parties. (In fact, his court was said to have been the dullest in Europe.) Surely he would never have gone anywhere near arsenic?

The answer is that his own doctors prescribed it to him. Poor George III regularly took a medicine made of antimony – a substance that contains the poison, arsenic.

So the very thing that was supposed to be making King George better was actually making him worse.

How mad is that?

More antimony, Your Highness?

Oh, you'll be the death of me, you know...

Crazy in love

John George IV, Elector of Saxony (1668 – 1694)

John George was very much in love.

Awww.

Unfortunately, the elector – a type of prince – wasn't in love with his wife, Eleonore; he was in love with his girlfriend, Magdalena.

Ah.

John George decided that it would be a really good idea to finish off his wife with a sword, so that he could marry his girlfriend instead.

Yikes.

He didn't succeed. The elector was foiled by his own brother, Frederick, who leapt to Eleonore's defence.

Hurray!

Unfortunately, Frederick was badly hurt.

Oh dear.

Eleonore survived ... but John George IV didn't. Two years later, both he and his girlfriend died of smallpox.

Shame.

The princess who swallowed a glass piano

Princess Alexandra Amélie of Bavaria (1826 – 1875)

Princess Alexandra didn't really swallow a grand piano made of glass, of course. She just thought that she had. The princess was convinced that she'd swallowed the glass piano when she was younger and that it was stuck inside her. So she was very careful when she walked in case she broke it. She also refused to wear anything but white. Whoever washed her clothes must have been thrilled about that.

BARMY RATING: 4 OUT OF 5

CAUTION
DO NOT EAT

Orange v Orange

Anna of Saxony (1544 – 1577)

The French noblewoman, Anna of Saxony was good-looking AND she had pots of money. This was a winning combination in the 16th century, as it meant that there was no shortage of suitable suitors. One of these was William I, Prince of Orange*, who was also known as William the Silent because he didn't, um, talk a lot.

Anna and William got married and went on to have five children together. Unfortunately the marriage wasn't a happy one. William of Orange said that his wife was bad-tempered and didn't care for their children properly. Anna poked fun at her husband in public. In short, they really didn't get on.

William banned Anna from spending her own money and then packed her off to live with his family so that they could keep an eye on her. So what did she do? She ran away. But William was so furious that he had Anna locked up, while ending their marriage on the grounds that she was mad.

Poor Anna died just six years later, imprisoned in two windowless rooms.

Meanwhile, William married twice more. And then he was assassinated in 1584, the first head of state ever to be murdered with a handgun.

Then he really was William the Silent...

Sob, there was no need to lock me away.

The 'Oranges'

Look, it's just not working anymore.

* The principality of Orange had nothing to do with oranges. It was a small state in the south of France.

CrackPot Quiz Question

Q. Did Countess Erzsébet Báthory of Transylvania...?

a) Bite her servants;

b) Punish a servant girl who talked too much by sewing her mouth closed;

c) Bathe in blood.

It is rumoured that Countess Erzsébet Báthory (1560–1614) did ALL THREE! Yikes. After being convicted of various atrocities, she was bricked up into a windowless prison with small holes left for water and food to be passed through. Unsurprisingly, she died in there.

MAD, BAD and truly sticky ENDINGS

Fools!

King Martin of Aragon (1356 – 1410)

It's never a good idea to eat an entire goose in one go. But King Martin of Aragon in Spain was a greedy guts who did just that. So it's hardly surprising that he then came down with a particularly nasty bout of indigestion.

Unfortunately, his favourite court jester picked just that moment to tell him a really funny joke about a deer that had been killed because it had been caught stealing figs.

(*Perhaps you had to be there.*)

Anyway, King Martin died laughing.

No, really. He actually died.

And that really isn't funny.

BARMY-O-METER

BARMY RATING: 3 OUT OF 5

The brick man of Babylon

Nebuchadnezzar II (634 – 562 BC)

Some people write their names on their stuff, so everyone else knows who owns it. So did Nebuchadnezzar II, king of the Neo-Babylonian Empire, who is famous for building one of the Seven Wonders of the Ancient World. Except it wasn't everyday stuff, like his pencil case or his geometry set. He wrote his name on bricks. Lots of bricks.

Seriously.

He didn't write
his name on every single
one, because that would have taken ages (and pen doesn't
write too well on clay). Nebuchadnezzar's baked bricks were
stamped with an inscription. This was either his name –
the long, fancy version – or a grand statement about the
fabulous thing that the brick was being used to build. And
as it's said that Nebuchadnezzar ordered the construction of
quite a lot of fabulous things during his lifetime, including
the Hanging Gardens of Babylon and the Ishtar Gate,
archaeologists have found his name **EVERYWHERE***.

* Except the North Pole, of course. That was quite a long way
from where he lived. And not in South America, where he didn't
live either. In fact, the bricks have been found mostly where the
Neo-Babylonian Empire once was, which is now in and around the
Middle East. But there were 15 million of them, which is quite a lot.

MADE-UP MONARCHS

Baron and Baroness Bomburst

Baron and Baroness Bomburst are truly the most bonkers, the silliest and definitely the oddest monarchs EVER. It's difficult to measure oddity, but think of the oddest monarch you can. And then multiply the oddness by 100. And then double it (because there are two of them).

That's the Bombursts. Odd with a capital 'O'.

But you mustn't worry about meeting them in real life, because they are completely fictional. (Phew.) You'll only see the Bombursts in the popular children's film *Chitty Chitty Bang Bang* (1968).

Baron Bomburst is a silly, spoilt, grown-up boy, while his wife the baroness is terrified of children. (She doesn't like

them much, either.) The Bombursts rule the totally made-up country of Vulgaria. But the castle in the film is VERY real and was built by Ludwig II, an actual Bavarian king (see page 40).

The film is based on the novel *Chitty Chitty Bang Bang*, by Ian Fleming. It's the story of mad inventor Caractacus Pott, who builds a magical car. But the Bombursts weren't in the original story. It was another author who added them when he wrote the actual screenplay for the film – an author whose jaw-droppingly fantastic characters are world famous. You may have heard of him. He's quite famous, too.

The author who invented the bonkers Bombursts was none other than the top children's author, Roald Dahl.

Ludwig II of Bavaria

MAD ABOUT...
HIGH HEELS (AND PANTS!)

Queen Catherine de' Medici of France (1519–1589)

If there was one thing the French Queen Catherine de' Medici hated more than being short, it was the idea of tripping and falling flat on her face in front of important royal guests, because more than ANYTHING ELSE the Queen of France hated looking like an idiot.

Her fear of falling over wasn't totally daft. In the 16th century, shoes had huge wooden soles that were difficult to walk in. So Catherine thought of a way of solving her height issues and her bad shoes in one go. She asked her cobbler to swap the wooden soles with slender heels, so that she didn't trip up when she entered the royal court. And because these were high heels ... she was now much, much taller.

Not content with changing the history of heels, Catherine's next fashion revolution was pants! Fed up of showing everyone her bottom when she climbed on and off her horse – because she and the rest of the ladies in her court did not wear anything under their frocks – Catherine started the fashion for wearing proper undergarments.

Did They Really Do That?

'I am most anxious to enlist everyone who can speak or write to join in checking this mad, wicked folly of Women's Rights. Feminists ought to get a good whipping.'

Whip them, I say!

Queen Victoria (1819-1901), speaking in 1870 on the subject of the Suffragettes, who fought for equal rights for women. Luckily, the queen's silly statement didn't stop the Suffragettes from continuing their campaign and women did get the vote.

Steady on, Ma'am!

CrackPot Quiz Question

Q. When George I of England's wife Dorothea died, did he...?

a) Go into deep mourning and wear black for the next 40 years;

b) Go mad with grief and insist that every female child born in England that year should be named Dorothea after his beloved wife;

c) Go to the theatre.

It's c). Dorothea was George's cousin as well as his wife. The marriage was arranged by their families and was not a happy one. When Dorothea fell in love with a Swedish count instead, George I (1660 – 1727) was livid. He divorced Dorothea and imprisoned her in a castle, where she remained until her death, over 30 years later. When he heard that Dorothea had died, it's said that George celebrated by going to the theatre.

And then he died, four weeks later.

Taa-dah!

Emperor Nero (37 – 68 AD)

Emperor Nero – or, to give him his full name,
Nero Claudius Caesar Augustus Germanicus
– wasn't your average ruler. He didn't just
sit on a throne and wear a crown and
laugh at the antics of a court jester. Oh no.
He was much more serious about power. He
was also utterly ruthless. If anyone stood in his
way, he simply got rid of them.

COURT
JESTER:
PLEASE
LAUGH!

NERO'S HIT LIST

Britannicus, Nero's stepbrother

When Nero's mother Agrippina tried to share
power with him, he said, 'NO'. Not to be outdone,
Agrippina tried to make her stepson – and Nero's
stepbrother – the emperor instead. So Nero
poisoned him.

Agrippina, Nero's mother

She just got in the way, really. To get rid of her, many suspect
that Nero arranged for her ship to be shipwrecked. But
Agrippina survived. So Nero had her executed instead.

Octavia, Nero's wife

Nero divorced Octavia on the grounds that she couldn't have children. Then he banished her to another country to make sure that she was properly out of the way. When the Roman people protested over his treatment, Nero relented and told Octavia she could come back. As soon as she returned, he had her executed.

Poppaea, Nero's next wife

Nero killed Poppaea and it's a wonder that anyone was brave enough to marry him after this, but Statilia Messalina did. Probably because Nero had already had her first husband executed. Hmm.

Next!

The city of Rome

Not a person, this time, but an **ENTIRE CITY**. Nero was famously blamed for setting Rome on fire and then playing his violin while it burned. However, historians are not convinced that he did it, especially as he actually played the lyre. But given his track record, it's not surprising that Nero got the blame for this anyway.

BARMY RATING: 4 OUT OF 5

Did They Really Do That?

Early to bed!

(By order of his majesty.)

William the Conqueror (1028–1087) introduced the curfew law in 1068. When the curfew bell was rung in the evening, everyone had to put out their fires and go to bed. Or else. But this wasn't quite as mad as it sounds. William didn't just want to make sure that everyone got a good night's sleep. The law was actually meant to stop his opponents getting together under the cover of darkness (no pun intended!) and planning to overthrow the king!

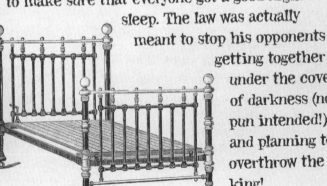

Fools!

MAD, BAD
and truly sticky
ENDINGS

William III of England (1650 – 1702)

William III wasn't killed by a spear while he was sitting on the toilet (like Wenceslaus III on page 16). He wasn't stabbed by a scheming bodyguard (like Emperor Caligula on page 52). He died because of a mole.

It happened like this ...

William's horse stumbled on a molehill, built by a mole.

The king fell off his horse and broke his collarbone.

Then he caught pneumonia.

And died.

All because of a mole*.

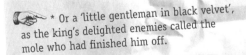

* Or a 'little gentleman in black velvet', as the king's delighted enemies called the mole who had finished him off.

Peter III of Russia (1728 – 1762)

Emperor Peter III was said to be witty, hot-tempered and sarcastic. And he simply adored uniforms. So was he mad too? Many said he was. Others disagreed. But there's one thing that everyone agrees on – he was definitely VERY royal indeed.

Born in Germany, Peter's grandfathers were Swedish and Russian emperors. After the poor lad was orphaned at the age of 11, his bossy guardians pointed him in the direction of the Swedish throne. All he had to do was marry into the Swedish royal family and he would become emperor.

# of sarcasm

yeah, right

Easy-peasy. Except his aunt – a Russian empress – had different ideas and whisked him off to Russia instead. In a trice, Peter's name was changed to Pyotr and before he could say, 'St Petersburg', he was named as heir to the Russian throne. When he was 17, he was told to marry a Russian princess. But she was a lot cleverer than him and they did NOT get on.

So was Peter mad or not? Who knows? As he was assassinated (probably by his own wife) only six months after he became emperor and when he was just 34, there wasn't really enough time to find out.

The royal shocker

KING CNUT NOT AN IDIOT AFTER ALL

We can (almost) exclusively reveal that King Cnut (985–1035) didn't really think he could hold back the tide. The king just did it to shut up his boastful courtiers, who were claiming that he was so great that he could command the tides of the sea to go back.

Cnut knew that there was no way he could do that. But he also knew that this was an opportunity to look good in front of his people. So he gave it a whirl anyway.

Below: an artists impression of the great day.

Cnut sat here

Crowds gathered here...

IT'S A RIGHT ROYAL READ!

The great day arrived

Cnut's people watched with bated breath as their king sat on his throne on the beach, with the sea creeping towards him.

What would happen?

Cnut, who knew exactly what was going to happen, was probably a bit more relaxed. And when the tide came in … and in … and in and he failed to stop the sea, Cnut was ready with a fabulous quote that he'd prepared earlier:

'Let all the world know that the power of kings is empty and worthless and there is no king worthy of the name save Him by whose will heaven and earth and sea obey eternal laws.'

Historia Anglorum, ed D E Greenway

Which basically meant that Cnut understood that kings were nowhere near as powerful as God.

So King Cnut got the chance to look wonderfully humble and religious in front of everyone, which makes him most definitely NOT an idiot.

Did They Really Do That?

A thoroughly royal campsite

Joseph I of Portugal (1714–1777) wasn't just scared by the terrible earthquake that hit Lisbon in 1755, killing 100,000 people. He was **TOTALLY FREAKED OUT BY IT!** Afterwards, terrified of aftershocks or further earthquakes, he refused to enter any of his palaces that were still standing in case they tumbled down on top of him.

Joseph's fear never went away. For the rest of his life, he hated being indoors. But he came up with a brilliant way of getting around this problem. He moved his entire royal court to the hills of Ajuda, where everyone lived in tents.

MAD, BAD

and truly sticky

ENDINGS

Fools!

Crown Prince Sado of Korea (1735 – 1762)

It is said that Crown Prince Sado wasn't a very nice chap and that he had a nasty habit of killing his servants. However, the way that his own father treated him wasn't exactly kind, either!

King Yeongjo ordered his servants to bring an empty rice chest. Then he sealed his son inside. **AND LEFT HIM THERE.**

When they opened the chest eight days later, Crown Prince Sado was dead.

Yikes.

Ok, Father. Good joke! Let me out now. Father...?

Silly Billy!

William IV of Great Britain (1765 – 1837)

William, Duke of Clarence never ever thought he was going to be king. (After all, he was third in line to the throne behind his two brothers. Surely they would have children who'd become king or queen next?) So he never ever bothered behaving in a particularly royal way.

He joined the Royal Navy, fought against the Spanish in 1780, took part in the American War of Independence, then came home, where he lived happily with an Irish actress and their 10 children. William had a reputation for being a bit wild, totally tactless, exceedingly eccentric and ridiculous too. So, because his name was William, he was nicknamed Silly Billy.

However, the tables were turned when he did become king after all at the grand old age of 64. It is rumoured that he said to the people who had once laughed at him, 'So, who's the Silly Billy now?'

BARMY RATING: 2 OUT OF 5

MAD ABOUT...
COLLECTING STUFF

King Farouk of Egypt (1920–1965)

Before he abdicated and left Egypt in 1952, spendaholic King Farouk built up amazing collections of rare and unusual things. He took 204 trunks of possessions with him, but had to leave most of his treasures behind, including...

Coins

King Farouk had about 8,500 gold coins and medals, including the really rare and super-expensive American 1933 Double Eagle coin. One of these coins was later sold at auction for over £5 million, making it the most expensive coin in the world.

Fabergé eggs

These aren't your average Easter eggs, but jewel-encrusted works of art that are worth a LOT of money. King Farouk owned two of them.

Stamps

King Farouk was the ultimate collector – a philatelist. (This means he collected stamps, not people called Phil.)

Nudes

These weren't real naked people, of course. It's not a good idea to collect those. They'd get really cold. But King Farouk did have a lot of paintings, sculptures and statues of the human body.

Cars

He owned more than 100 cars. If he could have found enough people to drive them, King Farouk could have made his very own traffic jam.

Toothpaste

After King Farouk left, the new occupants found piles of unopened toothpaste tubes inside his palace. That must have been a bit of a squeeze.

Oysters

King Farouk didn't actually collect oysters, because they would have gone off, but he is said to have eaten a staggering 600 of them every single week. He loved to feast on meat, fish, eggs and fizzy drinks, too.

Unsurprisingly, he was also very overweight. He died aged just 45 ... in a restaurant.

Fig. 103: Ostrea

One of the few oysters not to be eaten by King Farouk

Phew!

Rudolph II and the

Rudolph II, Holy Roman Emperor (1552 – 1612)

This isn't a magical tale of wizards with lightning-shaped scars. It's the totally true story of Rudolph II – the Roman Emperor who was a great fan of alchemy.

Er... what's alchemy?

> alchemy (n.) The science of turning base metals – such as iron, nickel, lead, zinc and copper – into glistening gold.

He also wanted to find the philosopher's stone.

Um... what's the philosopher's stone?

> philosopher's stone (n.) A legendary substance that is supposed to change any old metal into glistening gold.

To help him in his quest, Rudolph II invited top alchemists of the day to visit him. He hoped that together they would find the philosopher's stone, perform alchemy and create treasure troves of gold. He even had his own private alchemy lab for them to experiment in. So did he do it?

No he didn't.*

Philosopher's Stone

MADE-UP MONARCHS

The Emperor and his New Clothes

The Emperor's New Clothes tells the tale of an absurdly silly man, who was also an emperor.

It so happened that one day two weavers told the emperor that they could make him the most wonderful clothes ever. The best bit was that the fabric was totally and utterly invisible to anyone who was stupid.

The emperor thought this was a WONDERFUL idea. If he wore the weavers' amazing clothes, he'd be able to spot a fool anywhere. So he gave the weavers bags of money and asked them to start work at once. And so they did.

The problem was, the emperor couldn't see the clothes on the weaving loom. And when the weavers were finished, he still couldn't see them! Oh dear. Perhaps this meant that he was an idiot?

So he decided to pretend that he could see the clothes, so that he didn't look a fool. No one would EVER know.

He put the new clothes on and paraded through the streets, so that everyone could see how fabulous he looked.

But it wasn't just fools who couldn't see the emperor's new clothes. NO ONE could. And the reason that no one could see them was because the emperor was wearing NOTHING AT ALL. He'd been tricked, good and proper.

The royal joker

Christian VII of Denmark (1749 – 1808)

There was nothing Christian VII of Denmark liked better than a 'hilarious' practical joke.

He often slapped people around the face (presumably because they didn't dare slap him back?). Once, he even poured a bowl of sugar over his grandmother's head. But his favourite thing of all was playing leapfrog with visiting dignitaries. Whenever they bowed to him as a sign of their respect – over he'd go.

Boing!

What the...!

MAD, BAD
and truly sticky ENDINGS

Fools!

Adolf Frederick, King of Sweden (1710 – 1771)

The king of Sweden liked his food. A lot. For example, for his evening meal on 12 February 1771, he ate:

• One lobster.

• One dish of caviar.

• One heap of sauerkraut.

• One platter of smoked herring.

• And 14 helpings of his favourite pudding – semla* – which were served in 14 bowls of warm milk.

And then, because he'd eaten far, far too much, he died.

*A semla is a spiced bun filled with breadcrumbs, milk, marzipan, sugar and whipped cream. It's not low in calories.

Just the 14 bowls this evening, Your Majesty?

91

THE BARMY

634-562BC	Nebuchadnezzar II
6th cen. BC	**The Hanging Gardens of Babylon are built**
12-41 AD	Emperor Caligula
37-68 AD	Emperor Nero
10th century	The Grand Vizier of Persia
1028-1087	William the Conqueror
1066	**The Norman Conquest of England**
1206	**Genghis Khan becomes emperor of the Mongolian Empire**
1215	**The signing of the Magna Carta**
1215-1294	Kublai Khan, Emperor of Mongolia
1368-1422	Charles VI of France
1452-1485	Richard III of England
1455-1485	**Wars of the Roses**
1491-1547	Henry VIII of England
1519-1589	Queen Catherine de' Medici of France
1530-1584	Ivan IV Vasilyevich of Russia
1552-1612	Rudolph II, Holy Roman Emperor
1638-1715	Louis XIV of France
1649	**Defeat of the Spanish Armada**

TIMELINE

1668-1694	John George IV, Elector of Saxony
1672-1725	Peter the Great of Russia
1709-1762	Elizabeth of Russia
1710-1774	King Louis XV of France
1738-1820	George III of Great Britain and Ireland
1762-1830	George IV, The Prince Regent
1765-1837	William IV of Great Britain
☞ **1776**	**United States Declaration of Independence**
1789-1799	French Revolution
1793-1875	Emperor Ferdinand I of Austria
☞ **1803-1815**	**Napoleonic Wars**
1819-1880	Emperor Norton I of the USA
1819-1901	Queen Victoria
1845-1886	Ludwig II of Bavaria
☞ **1861-1865**	**The American Civil War**
1868-1918	Tsar Nicholas II of Russia
☞ **1917**	**Russian Revolution**
1920-1965	King Farouk of Egypt

POLITE NOTICE: entries labelled with the patented 'pointy finger' signify noteworthy historical events - thank you.

Index

TOTALLY HOOKED?

UTTERLY GRIPPED?

Then turn over to see our other fabulously bonkers titles...